★★★ KID ★★★
PRESIDENTS

TRUE TALES OF CHILDHOOD FROM
AMERICA'S PRESIDENTS

Copyright © 2014 by Quirk Productions, Inc.

Library of Congress Cataloging in Publication Number: 2013957088

ISBN: 978-1-59474-731-1

Printed in China

Typeset in Bell, Bodoni, Signpainter, Bodoni Highlight

Designed by Gregg Kulick
with Doogie Horner and Josh McDonnell

Illustrations by Doogie Horner

Illustration coloring by Mario Zucca

Production management by John J. McGurk

Quirk Books
215 Church Street
Philadelphia, PA 19106
quirkbooks.com

10 9 8 7 6

★ ★ ★ KID ★ ★ ★
PRESIDENTS

TRUE TALES OF CHILDHOOD FROM
AMERICA'S PRESIDENTS

STORIES BY **DAVID STABLER** ★ ILLUSTRATIONS BY **DOOGIE HORNER**

QUIRK BOOKS
PHILADELPHIA

TABLE OF CONTENTS

PART I

AFTER-SCHOOL ACTIVITIES

PART II

FANTASTIC JOURNEYS

PART III

IT'S NOT EASY GROWING UP

MEET THE
PRESIDENTS
═══ OF THE ═══
UNITED STATES

★ ★ ★ ★ ★ ★ ★

#1	GEORGE WASHINGTON	(BORN 1732)
#2	JOHN ADAMS	(BORN 1735)
#3	THOMAS JEFFERSON	(BORN 1743)
#4	JAMES MADISON	(BORN 1751)
#5	JAMES MONROE	(BORN 1758)
#6	JOHN QUINCY ADAMS	(BORN 1767)
#7	ANDREW JACKSON	(BORN 1767)
#8	MARTIN VAN BUREN	(BORN 1782)
#9	WILLIAM HENRY HARRISON	(BORN 1773)
#10	JOHN TYLER	(BORN 1790)
#11	JAMES KNOX POLK	(BORN 1795)
#12	ZACHARY TAYLOR	(BORN 1784)
#13	MILLARD FILLMORE	(BORN 1800)
#14	FRANKLIN PIERCE	(BORN 1804)
#15	JAMES BUCHANAN	(BORN 1791)
#16	ABRAHAM LINCOLN	(BORN 1809)
#17	ANDREW JOHNSON	(BORN 1808)

#18	ULYSSES S. GRANT	(BORN 1822)
#19	RUTHERFORD B. HAYES	(BORN 1822)
#20	JAMES A. GARFIELD	(BORN 1831)
#21	CHESTER A. ARTHUR	(BORN 1829)
#22	GROVER CLEVELAND	(BORN 1837)
#23	BENJAMIN HARRISON	(BORN 1833)
#24	GROVER CLEVELAND	(BORN 1837)
#25	WILLIAM MCKINLEY	(BORN 1843)
#26	THEODORE ROOSEVELT	(BORN 1858)
#27	WILLIAM HOWARD TAFT	(BORN 1857)
#28	WOODROW WILSON	(BORN 1856)
#29	WARREN G. HARDING	(BORN 1865)
#30	CALVIN COOLIDGE	(BORN 1872)
#31	HERBERT HOOVER	(BORN 1874)
#32	FRANKLIN D. ROOSEVELT	(BORN 1882)
#33	HARRY S TRUMAN	(BORN 1884)
#34	DWIGHT D. EISENHOWER	(BORN 1890)
#35	JOHN F. KENNEDY	(BORN 1917)
#36	LYNDON B. JOHNSON	(BORN 1908)
#37	RICHARD M. NIXON	(BORN 1913)
#38	GERALD R. FORD	(BORN 1913)
#39	JIMMY CARTER	(BORN 1924)
#40	RONALD REAGAN	(BORN 1911)
#41	GEORGE H. W. BUSH	(BORN 1924)
#42	BILL CLINTON	(BORN 1946)
#43	GEORGE W. BUSH	(BORN 1946)
#44	BARACK OBAMA	(BORN 1961)
#45	DONALD TRUMP	(BORN 1946)

INTRODUCTION

nce upon a time, a Virginia farm boy named George Washington was playing with a hatchet in his parents' garden. He came upon his father's favorite cherry tree, which he proceeded to chop and chop until the tree fell crashing to the ground. When George's father confronted him, George replied with words that have been duly recorded in history books ever since:

At that moment, a gust of wind arose and knocked the guilty boy off his feet. From out of the sky came a huge and mighty fire-breathing dragon.

The fearsome creature scooped up George and carried him off to its lair, in a magical land populated by flying pigs and winged monkeys. There George was adopted by a dragon family and treated with kindness.

Of course, that whole story is a fantasy, beginning with the part about the boy and the hatchet. Young George Washington never chopped down a cherry tree. He never said "I cannot tell a lie." That's just a story a pastor named Mason Weems invented in the early 1800s, and schoolbooks have been repeating it ever since.

The real George Washington was just a regular kid. In fact, every president in United States history started out like you and me. Sure, many of them grew up to achieve amazing things. But as children, they went to school, played sports, fought with their brothers and sisters, and did all the crazy things kids do.

So in this book we won't even pretend that George Washington chopped down a cherry tree. But we will tell you about the time he tried swimming across the Potomac River—and nearly drowned.

And you'll read about how a young John F. Kennedy was always fighting with his big brother Joe.

And you'll read about how a young Dwight Eisenhower dealt with bullies, older brothers, and a savage barnyard goose.

You'll read about how young Ronald Reagan over-came his bad eyesight, picked up a pair of glasses, and became the legendary lifesaver of Dixon, Illinois.

And you'll read about how, as a boy, Barack Obama moved to a new town in a different country and found his way—with some help from a friendly ape named Tata.

This is *Kid Presidents*, the book that proves any kid can grow up to be president. Because every U.S. president started out as a regular kid. Just like you.

So if you want to make your country a better place—and you're willing to work very hard—who knows where you'll find yourself someday? Maybe you'll go all the way to the White House, just like all of these crazy kids.

PART

ONE

AFTER-SCHOOL
ACTIVITIES

HORSES, BIOLOGY, THEATER AND MUSIC!

THE

KID PRESIDENTS

DISCOVERED ALL KINDS OF INTERESTING AND UNUSUAL HOBBIES

ULYSSES S. GRANT

THE HORSEBACK KID

=== BORN 1822 ===

He was the brave general who led the North to victory in the Civil War. In 1868, Ulysses S. Grant rode the fame he earned on the battlefield all the way to the White House. He may have been the gruffest, toughest president America ever had. You'd be tough, too, if you learned everything you know on the back of a galloping horse.

When Ulysses was a boy, a traveling circus passed through his hometown of Georgetown, Ohio. Back in the 1820s—before television, before movies, before radio—the arrival of a circus was a major event, especially in a rural village like Georgetown. The big top promised amazing acrobats, wacky clowns, death-defying trapeze artists, and all kinds of exotic animals. So, naturally young Ulyss (as he preferred to be called) rushed to watch the show.

When Ulyss arrived, the audience was admiring a beautiful but strong-willed pony in the center of the ring. The ringmaster stepped out to greet the audience and issued his challenge:

Ulyss raised his hand to volunteer, but a much bigger boy elbowed his way to the front of the line. The pony quickly threw the boy off, leaving him sprawled facedown on the sawdust floor.

So the ringmaster repeated his challenge.

Once more, little Ulyss volunteered. This time he was the one chosen, and a sea of hands lifted him onto the back of the miniature horse. Just as it had with the older boy, the pony did everything it could to shake off its rider. It reared up on its hind legs, pawing at the sky, but Ulyss seized hold of its mane, dug his heels into its flanks, and hung on.

At last the pony calmed and allowed Ulyss to guide it around the ring. The crowd roared with delight. When he had completed his circuit, Ulyss was hoisted aloft like a conquering hero, wearing a joyous smile on his face.

From that day on, Ulysses Grant couldn't get enough of horses: riding them, caring for them, training them. By the time he was five, he could ride standing up on the back of a trotting horse, holding onto the reins to keep his balance. By the age of seven, he had found a job hauling wood in a horse-drawn wagon. A neighbor expressed concern that little Ulyss could be trampled or kicked in the head if he wasn't careful.

But Ulyss's mother told her not to worry. "Horses seem to understand Ulysses," she bragged.

More than anything, Ulyss wanted a horse of his own. When he was eight years old, he finally found one to his liking. A farmer named Ralston was selling one of his colts, and Ulyss had saved up enough money from hauling wood to offer him $25. But Ulyss's father did not think the horse was worth that much. He instructed his son to offer $20. Then, if Ralston rejected the offer, Ulyss should offer $22.50. Only if Ralston held out for more was Ulyss to offer the full $25.

Ulyss raced over to Ralston's farm, eager to put his father's cunning plan into action. The cagy farmer grinned down at him. "So, boy, how much did your father tell you to pay?" he asked.

Ralston drew himself up and puffed out his chest. "I cannot accept a penny less than $25," he declared.

"Sold!" And though Ulyss got his colt, he learned a painful first lesson in horse trading: never let the other guy know how much you're willing to pony up.

When Ulyss's friends heard the story of his transaction with Ralston, they began making fun of him and taunted him with the nickname "Useless." Surely he was an imbecile for blurting out his best offer. Surely he would never amount to anything if he couldn't even manage a simple horse trade. Maybe he really was "Useless Grant" after all.

But Ulyss just ignored their name-calling. He kept the horse he bought from Ralston for four years, practicing day and night until he had mastered every aspect of riding and training. In that time his reputation among the townsfolk grew by leaps and bounds.

By the age of nine, Ulyss was being hired by farmers to "break" their unruly colts by riding them until they were tamed. When horses got sick with distemper, Ulyss was asked to care for them. He drew crowds by riding bareback through the center of town and performing acrobatic feats at full gallop. Each time the circus returned to town, the ringmaster would offer a prize for the most audacious display of trick horsemanship. Again and again, Ulyss always won.

One time the ringmaster even tossed a monkey onto the boy's shoulders during one of his breakneck rides. The monkey panicked, grabbing Ulyss by the hair and shrieking in terror. For a moment, it looked as if Ulyss might lose control of his mount. But he kept the horse under control until they finished their ride.

So it seemed that Ulyss was not so useless after all. In fact, many people in Georgetown began hiring him to drive them by horse and carriage to Cincinnati and Louisville—some cities were more than sixty miles away. Ulyss's love of horses gave him a chance to see the wider world beyond his hometown.

As he gained experience with horses, Ulyss became savvier with people as well. The next time he swapped horses with someone, he made sure to drive a hard bargain. He even managed to get the man to kick in $10 cash to seal the deal. When the colt in question got spooked by a barking dog on the ride home, nearly galloping over a 20-foot precipice, Ulyss knew just how to calm him: he removed a bandanna from his pocket, gently blindfolded the animal, and eased him away from the edge of danger.

Ulysses Grant never lost his special bond with horses. When he was seventeen years old, he enrolled at the United States Military Academy at West Point. While there he set a school high-jump record that stood for twenty-five years. "It was as good as a circus to see Grant ride," one of his fellow cadets recalled.

As a grown-up, Grant served in the Union army during the American Civil War and eventually rose to the rank of general. Despite the bloody and violent war raging around him, Grant would tolerate no cruelty toward animals. Once when he witnessed a man beating a horse, he ordered the man tied to a tree "for six hours as punishment for his brutality."

Ulysses S. Grant became president of the United States in 1869, and he made a priority of expanding the White House stables. During his eight years in office, he sheltered more horses than any other U.S. president. Because he never liked being driven around by a chauffeur, Grant often saddled one of his horses for a solo ride through the streets of Washington, D.C. One day, as he galloped his way down M Street, a police officer pulled him over for speeding!

When the officer discovered that the law-breaker was the leader of the country, he was embarrassed. But Grant wasn't the least bit upset. "I was speeding; you caught me," he said. So the police officer issued him a $5 ticket, and America's eighteenth president walked back to the White House on foot.

THEODORE ROOSEVELT

AND THE

BROADWAY SEAL

BORN 1858

They called him the Rough Rider, but he had a soft side as well. As president from 1901 to 1909, Theodore Roosevelt brought to the White House a zest for adventure and a love of the outdoors. No president did more to protect the environment than "T. R." Maybe that's because he grew up surrounded by wild animals.

Theodore "Teedie" Roosevelt was born into a wealthy family. He grew up in a beautiful brownstone mansion in New York City. One morning when he was about seven years old, Teedie's mother sent him to the market to buy strawberries for breakfast.

On his way up Broadway, the city's main commercial thoroughfare, Teedie pushed his way past hawkers, peddlers, and mongers selling all kinds of fish, meat, fruits, and vegetables.

And that's when he saw it. There, stretched out on a plank of wood, was the most mysterious creature Teedie had ever seen—six feet long and weighing nearly three hundred pounds, it had a dusty spotted coat that glistened in the morning sun.

A harbor seal! Teedie was mesmerized. He had never seen anything quite like it. The enormous creature looked like it belonged in the thrilling adventure stories he read at bedtime.

When he returned home that evening, he couldn't stop thinking about the seal. He wanted to see it again; he wanted to learn all about it. So, day after day, Teedie returned to the market to get another look. He brought a folding pocket ruler to measure the seal's length. To calibrate its girth, he had to maneuver the stiff wooden rule awkwardly over the creature's flabby body. Then he recorded every detail of the seal's anatomy in his notebook.

Teedie wanted to keep the seal for himself. He hoped to display it in a "museum" he was starting with two of his cousins. It would be an amazing museum with all the world's wonders on display.

But first he needed to convince the fishmonger to give him the seal . . .

Teedie asked and begged and pleaded—but it was no use. The fishmonger refused to give up his prize catch.

And then one morning Teedie returned to the market to find the creature was gone. Some lucky New Yorker would be enjoying seal steaks for dinner that evening (believe it or not, there was a time in New York when people ate seal for dinner).

Teedie was devastated. He couldn't believe he'd missed his chance. But the fishmonger recognized Teedie and called him over. He said he had a surprise for him. To Teedie's astonishment, the fishmonger reached underneath his table and pulled out the seal's skull.

Teedie was thrilled. The enormous skull was more than mysterious—it was absolutely out of this world! Stripped of its wooly blubber, it resembled the fossilized head of an ancient dinosaur. Who knew seals had fangs?! It looked ferocious, as if it might bite him at any moment.

The harbor seal skull became the first of many exhibits in the Roosevelt Museum of Natural History, for Teedie made good on his plan to become the world's youngest zoologist. The Roosevelt family's stately home was soon overrun with frogs, snakes, field mice, woodchucks, snapping turtles, and guinea pigs. Inspired by his encounter with the seal, Teedie learned how to skin and mount his animal specimens. And just as he did with the seal, he took detailed notes about each addition. He even catalogued the contents of their stomachs!

At first, Teedie kept his collection in his bedroom. But when a chambermaid complained to his parents, he was forced to move it into a bookcase he kept tucked away in a hallway.

When Teedie traveled, the Roosevelt Museum of Natural History went with him, much to the disgust of relatives who found themselves forced to share hotel rooms with tiny Teedie's roving taxidermy lab.

As Teedie grew older, his collection became too big for him to manage alone. When he was twelve, he donated part of it—a dozen mice, a bat, a turtle, four birds' eggs, and the skull of a red squirrel—to the American Museum of Natural History. Eleven years later, he presented 622 meticulously preserved bird skins to the Smithsonian Institution in Washington, D.C.

Teddy Roosevelt grew up to be one of America's greatest presidents. When he left the White House in 1909, he returned to his first love—the study and preservation of animals and their habitats. To recognize his efforts to save many animals from extinction, scientists gave several species the name *Roosevelti* in his honor.

PRANKSTER

★★★★ -IN- ★★★★

CHIEF

═══ SOMETIMES ═══

BAD KIDS

═══ GROW UP TO BE ═══

GREAT PRESIDENTS.

THESE FUTURE CHIEF
EXECUTIVES GOT A HEAD
START PLAYING DIRTY
TRICKS AT AN EARLY AGE.

★

ANDREW JACKSON liked to sneak out in the middle of the night, steal signposts, and move people's outhouses to where no one could find them.

||||||||||||||||||||||||||||||||||||||||||||||||||||||||||||||||||||||||||||||||||||||||||||||||

When he was eleven years old, JOHN TYLER led fellow students in a revolt against an especially strict teacher, Mr. McMurdo. They overpowered him, tied his hands and feet, and left him locked in a schoolhouse closet. It wasn't until late that night that a passerby heard the man's cries for help and freed him. The teacher immediately headed to Tyler's house to demand he be punished, but his father just replied with the Virginia state motto: *"Sic semper tyrannis,"* or, roughly translated, "That's what you get for being a tyrant!"

||||||||||||||||||||||||||||||||||||||||||||||||||||||||||||||||||||||||||||||||||||||||||||||||

One of **GROVER CLEVELAND**'s favorite pranks was to sneak into the school bell tower late at night and ring the bell, waking up all the townspeople. The first time he tried it, he accidentally locked himself inside the schoolhouse. He had to be let out and escorted home by his parents.

CALVIN COOLIDGE once locked a mule inside the classroom of a teacher he didn't like and left it there overnight. The next morning, the janitor heard a loud braying coming from the school's second floor. He unlocked the door and discovered the mule, which had taken the liberty of relieving itself all over the floor!

||||||||||||||||||||||||||||||||||||||||||||||||||||||||||||||||||||||||||||||||||||||||||||||||||||||||||||||

HARRY TRUMAN once tricked his cousin into believing he had an imaginary girlfriend. Fred Colgan and his friend Edwin Green were having a picnic on the banks of the Missouri River when they had idea to put a message in a bottle, float it downstream, and see if anyone replied. When Harry caught wind of their letter, he wrote a note of his own, signed it in the names of two imaginary girls from Mississippi, and sent it back by bottle to Fred and Edwin. The boys were excited to receive a reply and began corresponding with their new "friends." They mailed photos of themselves to an address that Harry gave them and even made plans to travel to Mississippi to visit their penpals. The prank went on so long that Harry's aunt had to order him to put a stop to it. Reluctantly, Harry informed Fred and Edwin that the girls to whom they had become so attached never really existed.

‖‖

JOHN F. KENNEDY once pulled a girl's hair so hard that she reported him to a policeman. When the officer came to the Kennedy home to investigate, John hid in his backyard until he went away. Another time, he changed the "No Dogs Allowed" sign on a restaurant to read "No Hot Dogs Allowed." He also liked to steal milk bottles from neighbors' porches and then sell them back for a few cents' profit.

‖‖

JIMMY CARTER convinced his younger sister to bury a nickel in the ground, telling her that it would grow into a money tree. Then, when she wasn't looking, Jimmy dug up the nickel and pocketed it for himself.

||||||||||||||||||||||||||||||||||||||||||||||||||||||||||||||||||||||||||||||||||||||||||||||||||||||||

GEORGE W. BUSH was the class clown. As a fourth grader, he grabbed a pen and drew a mustache, beard, and Elvis Presley-style sideburns on his face. As his class-mates erupted in laughter, George W. was frog-marched down to the principal's office for punishment.

RICHARD NIXON

AND THE

SIZE 9 BOOTS

OF DOOM

=== BORN 1913 ===

R ichard Nixon was the president of firsts. He was president when astronauts first walked on the moon, the first president to visit China, and the first president to resign from office. Before he got the chance to make history, however, he had to make his curtain call for the school play.

Young Richard Nixon (nicknamed "Dick" as a kid) was a shy and serious student—not the sort of boy you'd expect to sing and dance in theater productions. But all that changed when he met Ola Florence Welch, the daughter of a local police captain. Beautiful and outgoing, Ola was the opposite of Dick Nixon. As they began spending time together, she encouraged him to loosen up. She convinced him to take dancing lessons—he grumpily agreed he needed them—and to try out for his high school play.

In fact, Dick had a crush on Ola. He would have done almost anything to impress her—including enduring what was possibly the worst, most humiliating night of his life.

The trouble started when Dick agreed to a part in the school's production of *The Aeneid*, a classic play by the Roman poet Virgil. Dick had the starring role of Aeneas, the heroic Trojan warrior, and he had to dress in a toga. Minutes before the curtain went up, however, he realized that part of his costume was missing!

When he finally found the boots, he realized they were two sizes too small!

As the curtain rose, Dick was still struggling to pull the tiny boots over his big feet. Less than a minute to go before he made his dramatic entrance onto the stage! Two Latin teachers and a janitor hurried over to help him. With a little pushing and cramming and squeezing, they forced the boots onto Dick's feet. Heave ho!

But the boots were so tight, Dick could barely stand up. Still, he had to take his place on stage alongside the noble Queen Dido, played by the object of his affection: Ola. With every step, the too-small footwear pinched and chafed at Dick's oversized feet. As he was barking commands at his soldiers on stage, inside he was howling in pain. He was so uncomfortable that he could barely remember his lines (and just to make things extra complicated, he had to speak all of his lines in Latin!). The show was off to a terrible start.

And the performance quickly went from bad to worse. Kids hooted and whistled at Dick's big love scene with Ola. The two young actors stumbled over their lines. Were it not for the glare of the spotlights, the audience would have seen their faces turn red with embarrassment. But the show must go on, and somehow they got through it together.

Dick Nixon could have given up on acting that very night. Instead he persevered, as he always had, and that perseverance paid off. He appeared in many other plays over the years. In "Bird in Hand," he took the role of an English innkeeper. In "The Price of Coal," he played an elderly Scotsman. He sang and danced in the musical "HMS Pinafore." As a young man, he joined a theater group, the Whittier Community Players. At one lucky audition, he met his future wife—and America's future first lady—Patricia Ryan.

You have to be pretty persistent if you want to be elected president of the United States, and Richard Nixon surely carried the lessons of his disastrous early performance to the many speeches and appearances he would give on the way to the White House.

There was one other way that ill-starred school play changed Richard Nixon's life: He never wore boots again.

Richard Nixon ran for president three times—in 1960, 1968, and 1972. Every time he campaigned, he visited the state of Texas, where supporters often gave him cowboy boots as presents—at least ten pairs in all. He gave them all away because he could not stand to re-live the horror of that time back in school when he had to wear size 9 boots on his size 11 feet!

JIMMY CARTER

ARROWHEAD HUNTER

BORN 1924

Naval officer. Nuclear engineer. Peanut farmer. Jimmy Carter held a lot of different jobs before taking on the most difficult one of all, president of the United States, a post he held from 1977 to 1981. Behind that toothy grin was a serious man with a serious hobby. He loved collecting Indian arrowheads.

When Jimmy Carter was four years old, his family moved to a 360-acre farm in rural Archery, Georgia, where they grew cotton, peanuts, and sugarcane. Even at an early age, little Jimmy was expected to pitch in.

From sunup to sundown, he was busy with farm chores. He tidied the yard, gathered eggs from the chicken coop, fed the hogs in their pen, and tended the sweet potato and watermelon vines growing in the fields.

Jimmy's least favorite farm chore was "mopping the cotton"—a disgusting job that required him to smear cotton plants with a gooey bug-killing paste made from arsenic, molasses, and water. This homemade poison was so potent that it attracted loads of flies and honeybees. The insects would swarm around him since he was covered in the sticky sweet syrup.

Jimmy's favorite chore was climbing trees to help his mother harvest her pecans, a Georgia delicacy. Before long, Jimmy got a reputation as the best tree climber in Archery. Whenever the town's farmers went possum hunting, they sent Jimmy scurrying high up into the trees to shake the branches and dislodge their prey. Or that's what he was *supposed* to do.

As Jimmy's father, Earl, tended to his new farm, he began to learn about the Native Americans who once inhabited the western part of Georgia. When Earl discovered that Indians used to live on his property, he became even more curious about the history buried right under his feet. So he ran out and bought some books about Native American artifacts and how to find them. At night, he would read the books to Jimmy, who soon came to share his dad's fascination.

AND GOLDILOCKS SAID, "THIS ARROWHEAD IS FAR TOO BIG!" WHICH IS HOW SHE KNEW IT WAS APALACHEE, NOT CHEROKEE.

On rainy days, when work in the fields was impossible, Jimmy and his father would hike the land that Muskogee Indians had called home, gathering arrowheads and bits of shattered pottery. The best time of the year for finding Native American artifacts was early spring, after a long winter of storms, when every turn of a plow would churn up exciting new discoveries.

Over the years, Jimmy and his dad collected hundreds of Indian arrowheads. Jimmy liked competing with his father to see who could find the best and most interesting ones. Finding an especially beautiful "point," as the arrow tips are called, was a source of great pride for Jimmy. He was always eager to get back home and show his latest find to his family. Unlike other boys he knew, Jimmy never traded his arrowheads. He kept his collection intact.

Eventually, Jimmy left the farm to go to college. But he continued to scan the ground for Indian artifacts wherever he went—in city parks, on golf courses, along the well-traveled footpaths of university campuses. He was surprised to learn how plentiful these treasures were, if you knew how to look for them.

I THINK I SEE AN ARROWHEAD!

Later, when he became governor of Georgia, Jimmy got his wife, Rosalynn, and sons Jack, Chip, and Jeff to take up his hobby too. If they worked together, the Carters could cover an entire field in just a few hours. They'd line up and walk slowly, back and forth, stopping whenever someone saw a promising piece of flint. Sometimes all they found were broken rocks. Other times they got lucky. On one especially productive day they found twenty-six unbroken arrowheads—a family record.

After Jimmy Carter became president, he and Rosalynn would still return to Georgia for weekend retreats. While there, they spent hours walking hand in hand in the woods and fields searching for arrowheads. By the time he left the White House, Jimmy Carter had a collection of more than a thousand arrowheads. The oldest one was over twelve thousand years old.

Near the end of his term as president, Jimmy Carter signed a law that made it easier to hunt for arrowheads on public lands. As written by Congress, the bill would have banned arrowhead collecting altogether. But the president was determined to protect the hobby for future generations of Americans. He insisted on adding what came to be known as the "Carter Clause," which since 1979 has guaranteed that kids like him can continue to connect with history by collecting small pieces of it, one tip at a time.

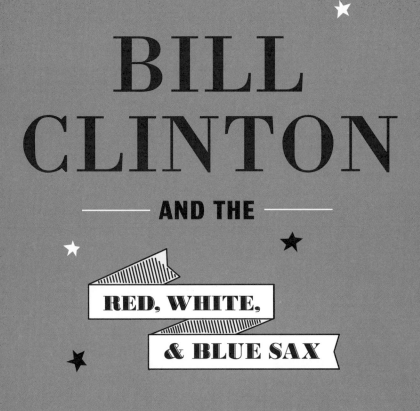

BILL CLINTON

—— AND THE ——

RED, WHITE, & BLUE SAX

=== BORN 1946 ===

Nobody liked being president more than Bill Clinton. In his two terms in office, from 1993 to 2000, he didn't just live in the White House. He filled it with his big, bold, colorful personality. The man they called "Bubba" enjoyed the spotlight and playing to the crowds— as some visitors learned the day they brought a saxophone to the Oval Office.

"Billy, will you be my Froggie?"

With these six words, Billy Clinton's life changed forever. He was the new boy at Ramble Elementary School in Hot Springs, Arkansas. Till then, he had been known more for his strange catchphrase—"Hot dog!"— than for his exploits in the classroom. But one day Billy was chosen to sing the part of Froggie in a performance of the old English folk song "Froggie Went a-Courtin'."

The song tells the story of a homely frog who asks a beautiful mouse to marry him. Playing the part of Miss Mousie was the prettiest woman Billy had ever seen: his fourth-grade music teacher. Entranced by the scent of her perfume, Billy swooned to the head of the class to begin their duet.

As he sang each line, Billy wasn't thinking about mice or frogs. He imagined he was courting the beautiful, sweet-smelling woman standing beside him.

Billy wasn't the only student who relished playing Froggie. All the other boys had a crush on their teacher too. But he took to the role with a gusto that few could match. From then on he was known as one of the most musical kids in his school.

Billy had discovered his love of music just in time. Like a lot of kids, he had trouble adapting to school. He was smart, but he talked too much in class, answering every question asked by his teachers—even the ones posed to other students. On his report card, he once got A's in every subject but a D for personal conduct.

"Billy, when you grow up, you're either going to be governor or get in a lot of trouble," one teacher told him. "It all depends on whether you learn when to talk and when to keep quiet."

Billy also struggled with his weight, which kept him from joining in a lot of games and sports. At the school Easter Egg hunt, he was the only one who failed to score an egg. He just couldn't get to them fast enough. Just when he'd find one, another kid would swoop in and grab it.

But Billy could do one thing better than almost anyone else: perform music. He especially loved the songs of Elvis Presley. He collected Elvis records and played them in his room for friends. He even styled his hair just like "The King." Sometimes, at parties, Billy would bring down the house with his hip-shaking Elvis impression. At last he'd found a positive way to stand out from the crowd.

The more Billy played and sang, the better he got. The better he got, the more opportunities he had to travel, make friends, and develop the leadership skills that would one day make him a president.

In junior high, Billy won awards for his saxophone playing. He performed at football halftime shows, marched in parades, and competed in band festivals across Arkansas. When he wasn't playing, he was practicing. Some days he played his sax for twelve hours straight, until his lips were so sore he could barely move them.

In summertime, Billy attended band camp at the University of Arkansas. It was there that he made another important discovery: being good at music not only made him feel better about himself, it also made other people feel better about him. Soon he was one of the most popular guys in town.

Thirty years later, in the middle of his first presidential campaign, Bill Clinton appeared on a popular late-night TV talk show. But he wasn't there to talk about politics. He was there to play the saxophone, electrifying the crowd with a rousing rendition of Elvis Presley's "Heartbreak Hotel."

Many people say that performance helped Bill Clinton take the lead in that year's presidential race. Without his killer sax solo, the American electorate may not have given the Arkansas governor a chance.

Bill Clinton seemed to agree. He once wrote: "I don't think I would have been president if it hadn't been for school music. Music has had a powerful influence on my life, helping me to learn how to mix practice and patience with creativity."

After he made it to the White House, Bill Clinton had less time for music. He had a country to run, meetings to attend, and fewer hours in the day to practice.

But one day in 1994, the head of a company that manufactured saxophones went to visit him in the Oval Office. He brought a ceremonial gift: a shiny new sax, custom made with red and white stripes, blue stars, and pearl keys. "I never thought I'd see a patriotic saxophone!" the president exclaimed.

Bill Clinton planned to donate the instrument to a music museum in South Dakota. But when the time came for Clinton to hand over the horn to the state's senators, he couldn't bring himself to part with it.

He ran through the scales he'd learned as a child and played a few of his favorite jazz tunes—until his staff members reminded the president to get back to work!

GAMES
PRESIDENTS
PLAY

BEFORE THEY WON ELECTION
TO THE WHITE HOUSE,
AMERICA'S FUTURE PRESIDENTS
HAD TO LEARN HOW TO
WIN ON THE PLAYGROUND.

SOME EXCELLED AT COMPETITION;
OTHERS WERE JUST
IN IT FOR THE SPORT.

As a boy, **BENJAMIN HARRISON** played an early form of baseball known as "town ball." In fact, he was quite the sportsman. An 1892 biography lists his athletic interests as "snow-balling, town-ball, bull-pen, shinny, and baste."

To defend himself against bothersome bullies, **THEODORE ROOSEVELT** took boxing lessons from a champion prizefighter named John Long. He became so good at brawling that he won a lightweight boxing tournament when he was just fourteen years old. The trophy was a pewter mug worth about fifty cents. It became one of Roosevelt's most cherished possessions.

WILLIAM HOWARD TAFT may have become America's heaviest president, but as a kid he was known to be light on his feet. He was an excellent baseball player, enjoyed ice skating, and even took dancing lessons twice a week.

WOODROW WILSON founded his own baseball team, the Lightfoots, and was elected its first president. He wrote a constitution for the club and presided over team meetings in his family barn. The team mascot was a large portrait of the devil ripped from a poster advertising deviled ham.

||||||||||||||||||||||||||||||||||||||||||||||||||||||||||||||||||||||||||||||||||||||||||||||||||||

GEORGE H. W. BUSH may have been the most competitive of all the U.S. presidents. "Our family's middle name was games," his brother Prescott once declared. The family's big backyard was the setting for epic touch football games in which George, Prescott, and their sister Dorothy all took part. In the winter, they used the yard as a makeshift toboggan run. When the weather turned really bad, they headed indoors for swimming races and ping-pong matches. They matched wits at the board game Parcheesi and the card games Go Fish and Sir Hinkam Funny Duster. Perhaps the most spirited Bush tradition was the family tiddlywinks tournament. One by one, the Bushes took turns to see who could launch the most small plastic disks—known as "winks"—into a cup. More often than not, the winner was George. He excelled at tiddlywinks, having figured out the secret formula for success: a special flick of the wrist that confounded his fellow players.

GEORGE W. BUSH (son of the above-mentioned George H. W. Bush) was mad for baseball. He could recite the starting lineups of every Major League team from memory. He kept a massive collection of baseball cards, many of which he mailed to players for their autographs.

When he lived in Indonesia, BARACK OBAMA played a game called kasti, which is similar similar to American baseball. Kasti is played with a tennis ball instead of a hard ball, the bases are called *hong*, and the players catch the ball with their bare hands instead of a glove. Barack Obama was known as an exceptionally courteous player. He used to field the ball and pass it to one of his smaller teammates, giving him the honor of throwing the runner out.

PART

TWO

FANTASTIC
JOURNEYS

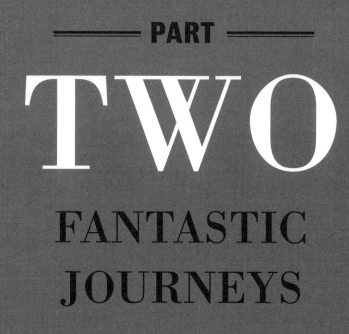

WILD FRONTIERS, DANGEROUS WARS, FOREIGN CULTURES, AND DISTANT LANDS!

THE KID PRESIDENTS

EXPERIENCED ALL KINDS OF

ADVENTURE

GEORGE
WASHINGTON

KID OF
THE WILD
FRONTIER

═══════ **BORN 1732** ═══════

America's first president was also one of its first heroes. The general who led the new nation's troops in its war for independence hoped to retire to his farm once the British were defeated. But whenever duty called, George Washington always answered. As a kid, that meant braving the Virginia wilderness to survey the land Americans would one day call their home. ★

Young George Washington watched as his two older half-brothers left their native Virginia to go to school in England. He always thought he'd follow in their footsteps, but then their father died when George was eleven. Now George would have to stay home and help his mother run the family farm. That wasn't the kind of life George wanted for himself, not at all.

Luckily for George, another person in his life had higher aspirations for him. His half-brother Lawrence was fourteen years older and an officer in the British army. George looked up to Lawrence. He was impressed by the officer's uniform, the gleaming scabbard at his side, and the dignified way he carried himself. Lawrence looked at his younger sibling and saw a miniature version of himself. With a little polishing, he thought, this rough-hewn farm boy could someday become an officer too.

In the summer of 1746, Lawrence arranged for George to sign on as a midshipman in the British Navy. George couldn't have been more excited. He packed his sea bag and hurried out the door to report to his ship.

Then his mother stepped in . . .

"Absolutely not," Mary Washington said. No son of hers was going away to sea, especially when she needed his help on the farm. She ordered George to unpack his bag and instructed Lawrence to find him a job closer to home.

George was devastated by his mother's decision. Now it seemed he would never leave the safety of the plantation. He moped around, dreaming of far-off places like the ones Lawrence had visited, convinced that he would never follow in his older brother's footsteps.

Then Lawrence came through with another brainstorm. His wealthy in-laws had purchased a parcel in the western Virginia wilderness, and they were sending about a dozen men to map the land. With his love of the outdoors and knack for mathematics, George was the perfect choice to help with the task.

George couldn't believe his good fortune. This mission might be even better than a sea voyage. All the adventure, all the camaraderie, but with zero chance of drowning—or so he figured. And because he would be gone for only thirty days, never even leaving Virginia soil, his mother could not object.

The expedition started out quietly enough. George recorded all of his observations in a small notebook that he'd titled "A Journal of My Journey over the Mountains." "Nothing remarkable happened," he observed on the second day of his journey. He spent most of the third day admiring the beautiful sugar trees that dotted the Virginia wilderness. For the next month, George kept an extensive diary, writing down every detail of his trek through the Virginia frontier.

With every passing day, the journey became more challenging. One night George discovered his bed was full of lice, fleas, and ticks.

Right then and there, George resolved to spend the rest of the expedition sleeping outside, in the open air, beside a campfire.

The very next day, it began to rain.

About a week in to the survey, the downpours were so bad that the Potomac River crested six feet higher than usual. George and his companions were forced to swim their horses to the other side. They emerged from the brackish water soaked to the bone.

I MIGHT END UP DROWNING AFTER ALL!

The next day, the surveyors continued their trip by canoe as another torrential storm buffeted them from the heavens. Finally, at about two o'clock in the afternoon, the skies cleared. That's when the Indians arrived.

WHY ARE THEY SOAKING WET?

BEATS ME.

There were about thirty of them, and George was terrified. He had never encountered a Native American war party before. What would they do? How would he defend himself if they were attacked? As the Indian visitors came closer, George realized they were more interested in dancing than fighting. The "war party" cleared a large circle and built a big fire in the center. Then they gathered around the fire and began to dance. A drummer kept the beat on a pot of water with a deerskin stretched tightly over top. George had never seen anything like it—and it was totally different than he had expected.

George would have many such experiences in his remaining days on the surveying expedition. He hunted wild turkeys, learned to cook over an open campfire, and even encountered his first "rattled snake."

When the expedition came to an end, George returned home convinced that the life of the outdoors was the life for him. The other members of the expedition had grown to like George. They spoke highly of him to other people, and eventually the lieutenant governor of Virginia invited George to join the militia. It was the begining of a long and glorious military career.

Many years later, as general of the armies in the American colonies' struggle for independence, George Washington led a small band of Revolutionary soldiers across the frozen Delaware River. He and his bedraggled men were forced to hunker down in makeshift huts during a long, wet Pennsylvania winter. These dangerous missions would have tested the mettle of even the greatest commander. But Washington was well prepared to survive such adversity because of the time he had spent as a boy on the wild Virginia frontier.

ANDREW JACKSON

THE LITTLEST PATRIOT

BORN 1767

T hey called him "Old Hickory" and that's what he was like: tough as the bark of a hickory tree. And just like bark, Andrew Jackson sometimes rubbed people the wrong way. He fought with anyone who got in his way during his two terms as president. Those who couldn't stand toe to toe with him quickly learned to step aside. Just ask the British soldiers he bested as a boy growing up in South Carolina.

He was the one kid nobody could bully. Sure, they tried. Andy Jackson seemed like an easy target. He was the new kid in town. Scrawny, freckle faced, and with an unruly mop of bright red hair, Andy stood out. He had a high-pitched voice; a childhood disability made him drool. But he refused to be pushed around.

From an early age, Andy liked nothing more than a good scrap. He was constantly getting into wrestling matches with other boys. Although he rarely won, he developed a reputation for toughness. "I could throw him three times out of four," one of his opponents remarked, "but he never stayed throwed!"

THIS KID
DOESN'T KNOW
WHEN TO QUIT!

URGH!
GIVE UP YET?
OOF!

Eventually, Andy would take on the biggest bully of them all—King George III of England.

In 1779, when Andy was twelve years old, troops loyal to the British king—called Tories—arrived in South Carolina to rid the land of American rebels who favored independence. The fearsome British commander "Bloody Ban" Tarleton and his Tory horsemen roamed the countryside around Andy's hometown, taking prisoners, seizing property, and laying waste to everything in their path. Andy's brother Hugh, one of the patriots who tried to beat back the British assault, was killed at the Battle of Stono Ferry.

When Andy heard the news, he vowed to avenge his brother's death. But when he tried to enlist in the militia, he was told he was too young. He had to wait a whole year until he was allowed to take up arms. His brother Robert signed up too. The two boys were issued pistols and musket rifles and sent out with the rebel forces.

One night, Andy and Robert were asked to stand guard at a farmhouse where an important patriot officer was spending the night.

In the morning, Andy saw Bloody Ban's mounted soldiers gathering for an attack. He pulled his pistol and fired a warning shot, giving the men inside a chance to escape. But then Bloody Ban's soldiers started coming directly for him and Robert!

Outnumbered and outgunned, the Jackson brothers were forced to retreat. Leaving their muskets behind, they headed into the deep woods behind the farmhouse.

For the next few days, Andy and his brother hid in the vast forest. It was a lot like a camping trip—except they didn't have tents, sleeping bags, food, or fresh water. They survived by eating nuts and berries. They slept underneath trees and rocks, and they often had to flee the British troops searching the forest.

Of course, even two very smart kids were no match for an entire army of British soldiers. The boys grew weaker and weaker. Eventually they were captured and hauled back to the farmhouse as prisoners.

When they arrived, they found the place in shambles. British soldiers had stolen all the valuables they could find and broke what they could not carry. Bloody Ban had returned to the comfort of his headquarters, leaving an especially cruel lieutenant in his place. He barked orders at them:

Andy and Robert did as they were told. The officer then commanded Andy to clean his muddy boots. But Andy, who had never backed down from a fight, refused to comply. He looked the man square in the eye.

The officer flew into a rage. He drew his sword and struck at the helpless prisoner. Fortunately, Andy was experienced in the art of self-defense. He threw up his hand to protect himself and managed to fend off the brunt of the blow. The sword cut a deep gash on Andy's forehead, leaving a scar that he would carry for the rest of his life.

The British soldiers were tempted to execute Andy on the spot, but they forced him into service instead. They ordered him to lead them to the house of another troublesome rebel named Thompson. Andy agreed, but he had a trick up his sleeve. Instead of taking his captors via the most direct route, he chose a circuitous road that could be seen a half mile from Thompson's front window. When the British soldiers finally arrived, they discovered Thompson had already fled—with a half-mile head start—thanks to Andy.

The soldiers were sick of being fooled by this thirteen-year-old upstart. They stripped Andy and Robert of their jackets and shoes and forced them to march forty-five miles—barefoot—to a prison camp at Camden, South Carolina. The brothers were not allowed any food. The only drink came from the rain that pounded them for the entire trip.

When they arrived at the prison, the brothers were penned up in a large cell packed with other captured patriots. No one had blankets; there was no medicine and precious little food. Baths were unheard of. The whole place stunk.

The unsanitary conditions soon caught up with the Jackson boys. Both contracted smallpox, a contagious and often deadly disease. Robert's face broke out in spots, and though Andy's case was not as dire, he feared that he too would succumb to the so-called Speckled Monster. Suddenly, death in prison seemed a very real possibility.

But Betty Jackson had learned of her sons' capture and hurried to Camden to beg the British to let them go. Released into her care, the gaunt and feverish boys were slung over two horses and rushed home in another driving rainstorm. It was a miracle they survived.

Andy managed to recover from his illness, but Robert was not so lucky. He died two days after they arrived home. Even worse, Andy's mother came down with smallpox too and soon passed away. Barely fourteen years old, Andy Jackson was now a war hero, a wounded veteran, and an orphan.

For the rest of his life, Andrew Jackson harbored a grudge against the British for the losses he suffered as a boy during the Revolutionary War. When the two sides squared off again, in the War of 1812, Jackson settled the score by leading the American forces to a decisive victory in the Battle of New Orleans. Dubbed "Old Hickory" for his tough-as-tree-bark reputation, he rode a wave of fame all the way to the presidency in 1829.

As U.S. president, Andrew Jackson continued to defy authority and pick fights with anyone who disagreed with him. His combative nature won him lots of passionate followers—and many bitter enemies as well. One thing his allies and adversaries agreed on was that he would never back down from a fight—a lesson the bullies of his boyhood had learned long ago.

MISHAPS HAPPEN

★ ★ OOPS! ★ ★

EVEN FUTURE PRESIDENTS
MAKE MISTAKES.

HERE ARE SOME OF THE
BIGGEST CATASTROPHES
THE KID PRESIDENTS
SURVIVED ON THEIR WAY
TO THE WHITE HOUSE.

The first time he tried to put on a pair of pants, **RUTHERFORD B. HAYES** stumbled and fell into hot coals.

HERBERT HOOVER once ate nothing but pears for two whole days. He got so sick that he refused to eat another pear for more than thirty years.

I SHOULD'VE STOPPED AT PEAR NUMBER 231!

HARRY TRUMAN broke his collarbone while combing his hair. (He fell off his chair.) Another time, he slammed a cellar door on his foot and accidentally

sliced off the tip of his left big toe. Fortunately a doctor was able to reattach it.

DWIGHT EISENHOWER accidentally
stabbed his brother in the eye with a whittling
knife.

RICHARD NIXON conked one of his best
friends on the head with a toy hatchet. He
was angry because the boy caught more
tadpoles than he did. The boy carried a
scar for the rest of his life.

JIMMY CARTER shot his own sister in the
backside with a BB gun after she threw a
wrench at him.

When BILL CLINTON was a kindergart-
ner, he broke his leg jumping rope. The
rope wasn't moving, just hanging limply between a tree and a swing set. All the other
kids had no problem clearing it, but heavy-

set Billy was wearing cowboy boots and couldn't get any lift. His heel caught on the rope, he went crashing to the ground, and he broke his leg. For the next two months, he lay flat on his back in a hospital bed with his leg suspended. When he went home, his parents bought him a present: a brand-new bicycle. But Billy wouldn't ride without training wheels for fear he would topple over and reinjure himself. He did not ride a bike again until he was twenty-two years old.

I GUESS COWBOYS SHOULDN'T PLAY JUMPROPE...

GET WELL

HERBERT HOOVER

BOY OF THE OSAGE

=== BORN 1874 ===

When he became president in 1929, Herbert Hoover was beloved around the globe for his efforts to feed the world's hungry. But he had the bad luck to take office just as the Great Depression hit—and many Americans blamed him for it. That's too bad because he could have been a great president. He had the brains, the skills, and a can-do spirit that he learned from the Native American friends he made as a kid.

Herbert Hoover was destined for greatness. That's what his father thought, anyway. "Another General Grant is born!" Jesse Hoover proclaimed the day his second son came into the world, in 1874. Nobody else in West Branch, Iowa, thought Bertie Hoover was destined for anything but a dunce cap, however. As a boy, Bertie was terribly accident prone. He once nearly chopped off one of his own fingers while playing with an axe. Another time, he got mired in mud while crossing a dirt road near his house.

Bertie and fire were also a volatile mix. His father worked as the town blacksmith, and Bertie liked to visit the smithy and watch him shoe the horses. One day he traipsed across the floor in his bare feet and stepped on a burning ember. The resulting scar remained with him for the rest of his life.

When he was five, Bertie accidentally started a fire when he plunged a red-hot branding iron into a pot of scalding tar. Neighbors came running to put out the blaze, which filled the skies with thick black smoke.

But Bertie did some things well. He loved the outdoors. He and his father enjoyed fishing and swimming. In the winter, they would slide down the snow-covered hills on a homemade sled.

Bertie would have learned to hunt too, but his parents were Quakers—members of a religious movement that didn't approve of guns.

Unfortunately, when Bertie was six, his father died of a heart ailment. His mother had to work several jobs just to keep food on the table. In the end, she decided it was best to send the children to live with her relatives in different states. So in the summer of 1881, Bertie traveled by train and then buggy to stay with his uncle, Major Laban Miles, who lived with the Osage Indians in Pawhuska, Oklahoma. It was the first time Bertie left Iowa—and it was a very long ride.

It was also his first time living among Native Americans. Uncle Laban was an Indian agent, appointed by the president to act as a mediator between the Osage and the U.S. government. For the next eight months Bertie lived, went to school, and played among the Osage boys and girls.

From his Indian friends Bertie learned how to make a bow out of Osage orange wood and shoot an arrow. Now he could finally hunt without a gun!

Bertie took the opportunity to learn everything he could from his companions. They went to Sunday school together, camped out in the woods, and fished in nearby streams. Sometimes it was hard to communicate, so Bertie bridged the gap by learning to speak some of the Osage language. Little by little, they figured out how to understand one another.

The Osage showed Bertie how to build a campfire, identify edible plants, and hunt for interesting rocks in the vast flat lands that surrounded the reservation. They shared stories from their culture and taught him to respect a way of life much different from his own.

After eight months, Bertie left Oklahoma and returned to live with his mother, but he never forgot what his Native American friends taught him. He carried his knowledge of rock hunting to his new home, studied geology in college, and became a mining engineer.

When Herbert Hoover ran for president in 1928, he made Charles Curtis, a U.S. senator of Osage ancestry, his running mate. They won in a landslide.

In the White House, President Hoover worked hard to improve the living conditions and promoted the self-sufficiency of American Indians. A major component of his "Indian policy" was the idea that the best way to ensure the survival of the Native way of life was by exposing it to the wider American culture. That was something Herbert Hoover and Charles Curtis knew firsthand.

FRANKLIN D. ROOSEVELT

AND HIS

DAY OF FREEDOM

BORN 1882

In the 1930s, when the economic collapse known as the Great Depression brought America to its knees, Franklin D. Roosevelt helped put the nation back on its feet. "The only thing we have to fear is fear itself," he famously declared. So how did a spoiled rich kid get to be such a courageous president? First he had to learn to stand up for his own freedom.

The future president of the United States sat on a crate, gazing obediently at the camera. His blonde hair flowed softly over the shoulders of a frilly white dress. In his tiny hands he held a feathered bonnet. The hem of his skirt spread out demurely just below his knees. On his feet he wore a pair of black patent leather shoes. In an instant, the light above the camera flashed—*POP!*—and forever captured two-and-a-half-year-old Franklin D. Roosevelt's image just as his mother wanted to remember him: dressed like a girl.

In those days, it wasn't unusual for boys to wear dresses for formal photographs. In fact, it was considered fashionable. But eventually young Franklin reached the age when he wanted to cut his hair short and to dress like other boys, and that's when the trouble started. His mother, Sara Delano Roosevelt, cried when the barber cut off his beautiful golden curls. She agreed to put away the dresses only if Franklin would agree to wear a miniature navy blue sailor suit. In the Roosevelt house, this was considered a grand compromise.

She simply refused to let him wear the clothes he wanted to wear—or to do many of the things he wanted to do.

I FEEL SO MANLY.

SOMEDAY A PRINCESS WILL KISS ME, & I'LL BECOME A REAL DUCK...

Franklin's mother managed every moment of her son's day: He woke up at 7 a.m. He ate breakfast at 8. He took his lessons from 9 to noon. Then he ate lunch. He was allowed an hour for play, followed by more lessons until 4 p.m. After that he was allowed two more hours to play games that his mother approved of before supper was served at 6 p.m. Two hours later, at 8 p.m., Franklin was put to bed. The same schedule was observed day after day, month after month, year after year.

Monday – Sunday

7 AM	8 AM	9–12 PM	12 PM	1 PM
$+\ \dfrac{1}{3}\ \dfrac{=4}{0}\ \overset{8}{\underset{\div}{\times}}$				RETURN TO START
2–4 PM	4–6 PM	6 PM	8 PM	

Franklin also had no privacy. His mother followed him everywhere. Once, when Franklin came down with scarlet fever, the doctor banned all visitors from his bedside. But his mother would not be denied. She leaned a ladder against the side of the house so that she could climb up and peep in on her son through his bedroom window.

Wary about letting her only child fall in with the wrong crowd, Sara insisted on selecting Franklin's playmates. Few neighborhood kids wanted anything to do with the strange rich kid whose mom was constantly hovering over him. Sara was reduced to begging children to come over and play with Franklin. When she couldn't find anyone, he would bang his head against the wall in frustration.

But if playtime was bad, bathtime was worse. Franklin wasn't allowed to bathe by himself until he was almost nine years old. That brief taste of freedom was enough to prompt him to write home in triumph to his father from his grandmother's house: "Mama left this morning, and I am to take my bath alone!" The very next day, Franklin's mother went back to overseeing his tub time.

Eventually, this maternal overprotection began to take a toll. Franklin loved his mother very much, but he felt like he never had any solitude or independence. It's totally normal to want to be alone with yourself, but his mom didn't seem to understand.

One day she found Franklin sitting all alone, looking sad. She did what she could to cheer him up, but he remained stuck in a melancholy funk. "Are you unhappy?" she asked. Franklin paused. Then he lifted his head and replied with great weariness: "Yes, I am unhappy." When his mother asked why, Franklin was silent again for a moment. He clasped his hands and struggled to explain that he needed a little freedom.

His mother was shocked. She had never seen her son so despondent. What did it mean? She asked Franklin what he would do if he had complete freedom. He said he didn't know. But clearly it was something that was very important to him.

The next morning, Franklin's parents took him aside. They told him that, for one whole day, he could do whatever he desired. He could ignore his daily schedule, disobey every rule his mother had laid down, and go anywhere he wanted, doing whatever he pleased. Needless to say, Franklin was ecstatic!

Almost immidietly, he ran out the door.

And didn't return until late that night—hungry, tired, and covered in dirt.

Franklin didn't say a word about where he had been or what he had done. His parents were mystified.

Was he out wrestling a bear?

Was he running atop a moving train?

Did he foil a bank robbery?

Was he trampled by a herd of angry Bigfoots?

No one ever found out. In fact, for the rest of his life, Franklin D. Roosevelt kept the secret of his "Day of Freedom" all to himself. He never told anyone in his family, not even his wife, Eleanor, where he went that day.

But we can't help but wonder if the Day of Freedom unleashed something special in Roosevelt. Perhaps the taste of autonomy sparked something that allowed him to become a strong, independent person who would one day be elected president of the United States.

BARACK OBAMA

NEW KID IN TOWN

BORN 1961

When elected in 2008, Barack Obama made history. He was the first black man, and the first "skinny kid with big ears and a funny name," as he put it, to become president of the United States. Being the first anything is never easy, as Obama would learn during his two terms in office. But he was prepared for it. After spending his boyhood in Indonesia, he knew a little something about being the new kid in town.

The moment he walked through the front gate of his new home, little Barry Obama knew one thing for sure: he wasn't in Honolulu anymore.

For starters, a huge hairy animal was ready to hop onto his shoulders. The creature was high in the treetops of Barry's new front yard, perched on a branch and howling at him. Amazed, Barry turned to his mother, who was equally surprised.

LOOK MOM, A MONKEY!

ACTUALLY, I'M A GIBBON

"His name is Tata," explained Barry's stepfather, Lolo Soetoro, who owned the house and the swinging simian guest.

Stepping into the ape's enormous shadow, Lolo paused to feed it a peanut from his pocket. Then he turned to his stepson. "I brought him all the way from New Guinea for you!"

Barry knew that his stepfather had a job drawing maps for the Indonesian army, and that his work took him to some strange and faraway places. But he had no idea that Lolo had returned from one of his trips with such an unusual welcome-home gift.

Barry leaned forward to examine the ape. Tata, however, was not in a welcoming mood. He looked like he was about to lunge forward, so Barry backed away.

"Don't worry," Lolo reassured him. "He's on a leash." He gave Tata another peanut and then gestured for Barry and his mother to follow him into the backyard. "Come," he said. "There's more."

This new place was a big change for Barry. Back in Hawaii, he had lived with his grandparents in a four-bedroom home in one of Honolulu's prettiest neighborhoods.

His new house, on the volcanic island of Java, was in a ramshackle neighborhood on the outskirts of town. Half the people in the capital of Jakarta lived in old bamboo huts. Electricity had come to the residents only a couple years earlier.

To get to his new house, Barry had to cross a narrow rickety bridge over a wide brown river. Below he could see children riding water buffalo and villagers washing their clothes in the muddy water.

GOOD MORNING!

Barry felt like he had traveled to an exotic and distant land. Things went from strange to stranger when he followed Lolo into the backyard.

From the looks of the place, you might have thought Lolo was a zookeeper. Animals emerged to greet them from all corners: chickens and ducks, a snake, an iguana, even a turtle the size of a cookie tin. A large yellow dog howled. A big white cockatoo screeched. Two brilliantly colored birds shook their long tail feathers. Barry would soon learn they were called birds of paradise and could be found all over New Guinea. Lolo explained that his travels allowed him to pursue an unusual hobby: collecting unusual animals.

The strangest creature of all resided in a concrete tub, about a foot and a half deep and a yard long that was half submerged in a small pond fenced off by chicken wire. Green and scaly, it looked like a cross between a dragon and a crocodile. The Indonesians knew it as a biawak, or monitor lizard, a venomous meat eater that liked to feast on crabs, squid, and fish. As Barry peered into the tub, he made a frightening discovery. There wasn't just one lizard. There were two!

As the only foreign child in the neighborhood, Barry was teased more than any other kid. His appearance also made him stand out. He was chubby, with dark skin and curly hair. At school, he was known as "the Little Duck" because of the way he waddled when he ran.

It didn't help that Barry couldn't speak the Indonesian language. For the first few months, he spent most of his time sitting by himself in the back of the classroom, drawing Superman and Batman in his notebook. But after just six months, he had learned the language and could communicate with the other children.

Sometimes the other kids would play pranks on Barry. They'd offer him something he was familiar with from America, like chocolate. But when he bit into it, he found that it was shrimp paste. Another time they gave him red hot cayenne peppers and told him it was candy.

One day Barry tagged along with a group of his school friends on a visit to the local swamp. When they arrived, some of the other boys seized him by his hands and feet. They picked him up and began to swing him back and forth. "One…two…three!" they yelled, and threw him into the water.

What they didn't know was that Barry had learned how to swim in Hawaii. Paddling furiously, he managed to escape the murky waters by himself.

Barry never felt totally comfortable living in Indonesia. It would always remain a somewhat scary place where he didn't quite fit in. But he learned to adapt, finding ways to make it feel more like home. Learning to speak the local language was one way.

Standing up for himself when teased was another. Barry joined the scouts, taught himself to sing local patriotic songs, and even studied karate.

He also stopped hiding in the back of the class and moved up front, where he became well known among his teachers for always shouting out the right answers.

Whenever he encountered an aspect of Indonesian culture that puzzled or surprised him, Barry would write a letter to his grandparents back in Hawaii. He would tell them about the people he met or the unusual foods he ate—like roasted grasshoppers and crispy fried crickets. In return, they would send him packages of familiar treats from America, like peanut butter and chocolate. But not every detail made it into his letters. Some things he saw, like the extreme poverty and disease that afflicted many villagers, were just too difficult for him to put into words.

1. ROASTED GRASSHOPPER

2. RAT

3. CRISPY CRICKETS

After four years in Jakarta, Barry was no longer the new kid in town. He had learned to survive new surroundings. But he was still homesick. His mother, Ann Dunham, realized that he would be happier back in Hawaii. She also worried about his future growing up in such a poor and turbulent country. So when Barry was ten, Ann and Lolo put him on a plane to Honolulu and sent him to live with his grandparents. It was just the next stop on a long journey that would take Barack Obama on to Los Angeles and New York, then from Boston to Chicago, and eventually all the way to the White House.

Sometimes you have to leave a place before you really begin to appreciate it. In later years, Barack Obama would remember his time in Indonesia as "one long adventure, the bounty of a young boy's life." He always cherished the memories of his childhood, even when he became president of the United States.

HARDLY WORKING

NO MATTER HOW OLD YOU ARE,

★ WORK CAN BE A PAIN. ★

SOME KID PRESIDENTS TRIED TO
AVOID DOING CHORES AT ALL COSTS.

OTHERS FOUND WAYS OF
TURNING THEIR CHILDHOOD
JOBS INTO MONEYMAKING
OPPORTUNITIES.

★ KA-CHING! ★

JOHN ADAMS hated studying. When he complained to his father about schoolwork, he was told to try digging ditches instead. The next morning, John headed out to the meadow and spent the entire day scooping up sod. It was sweaty, muddy, backbreaking work and it left the boy sore, hungry, and thirsty. The next day, he returned for another shift, attacking the ditch with his shovel from dawn to dusk but making little progress. That night, he went home and told his father he was through digging ditches and wanted to go back to his schoolwork.

THIS IS WORSE THAN STUDYING LATIN!

His father happily agreed. "If I have since gained any distinction," Adams later recalled, "[it's because of my] two days' labor in that abominable ditch!"

||||||||||||||||||||||||||||||||||||||||||||||||||||||||||||||||||||||||||||||||||||||||||||||||||

As an eighteenth-century farm boy, JAMES MONROE had his share of unpleasant chores to perform. The one he hated most was plucking goose feathers for use in pillows, mattresses, and quilts. The enraged geese tried to bite him every time he yanked one of their downy feathers.

||||||||||||||||||||||||||||||||||||||||||||||||||||||||||||||||||||||||||||||||||||||||||||||||||

When he was fifteen years old, RICHARD NIXON got a job plucking chickens in a butcher shop.

||||||||||||||||||||||||||||||||||||||||||||||||||||||||||||||||||||||||||||||||||||||||||||||||||

At the age of five, pint-sized entrepreneur JIMMY CARTER began selling bags of boiled peanuts on the streets of his hometown. He sold small bags for a nickel, jumbo bags for a dime, earning about a dollar a day. The experience taught him how to judge a person's character. "The good people were the ones who bought boiled peanuts," he said. "The bad ones didn't."

BARACK OBAMA's first job was scooping ice cream at a Baskin Robbins. He has hated ice cream ever since.

PART
THREE

IT'S NOT EASY
GROWING UP

BULLIES,
BAD EYESIGHT,
BIG
BROTHERS,
AND ANGRY GEESE!

THE
KID PRESIDENTS

OVERCAME ALL
KINDS OF
OBSTACLES

ABRAHAM LINCOLN

AND THE

NOT-SO-WICKED STEPMOTHER

BORN 1809

When civil war threatened to tear America apart, this great president held the union together. Abraham Lincoln came from humble beginnings—he really was born in a log cabin—but his love for learning allowed him to grow into one of the wisest leaders the United States has ever known. Long before he united North and South, however, he helped reconcile his own family.

The Lincoln family moved to the untamed settlement of Little Pigeon Creek, Indiana, when Abe was just seven years old. Bears, wolves, and other wild animals roamed the woods near his house. Sometimes Abe had to help his father kill animals for food. The meat filled their bellies, and the pelts kept them warm during the long frigid winter.

Even more dangerous than encounters with wild animals was the threat of contracting a deadly disease. Illnesses with scary names like ague, typhus, and the trembles could wipe out an entire settlement. You could get sick without knowing it, sometimes just by eating the wrong thing. That's exactly what happened to Abe's mother, Nancy. She ate the meat of a cow that had grazed on a poisonous plant and came down with a disease called milk sickness. A few days later, she died. Abe was just nine years old; his sister Sarah was only eleven. Both of them missed their mother terribly.

It took a long time for the Lincoln family to get over her death. An entire year passed. During that time, their cabin, which had always been a bit ramshackle, fell into disrepair. Snow cascaded through a hole in the roof, mounding in the loft where Abe slept. Wind whipped in through the moth-eaten bearskin that served as a door. Abe and his sister were forced to sleep on a floor covered with corncobs and straw. Their life in Little Pigeon Creek had never been easy, but now it seemed like they were worse off than ever.

Their father, Thomas, wasn't doing so well either. He was lonely without his wife, and he longed for a companion to help him raise his children. In the autumn of 1819, Thomas told Abe and Sarah that he was going back to Kentucky to look for a new wife. He even had an idea whom she might be: Sarah Bush Johnston, a child-hood friend, who had recently lost her husband and was raising three kids by herself.

Abe and his sister nervously awaited their father's return. Thomas was away for three weeks, leaving the children alone to face the onset of winter—and many questions about their new mother. What would she be like? Would she favor her own children over them? Would she be a cruel and wicked stepmother?

Abe prepared for the worst, worrying right up until the day a covered wagon drawn by four horses arrived at the cabin door. Out of it stepped a smiling Thomas Lincoln, followed by three small children and a big-boned, rosy-cheeked woman with a kindly face.

Abe eyed the woman warily. She looked pleasant enough, and she was certainly warm to the touch. When she gathered Abe close, he felt like a little chick being taken under the wing of a soft-feathered bird. But could Abe trust her? He had gotten used to looking out for his big sister while Father was away, and he wasn't about to let anyone come between them.

Well, one thing was for sure: it was about to get a lot more crowded in the cabin. The belongings Sarah brought from Kentucky filled the entire four-horse wagon. When Abe pitched in to carry some of them, he was amazed by what he saw: a spinning wheel, a featherbed with feather pillows, a beautiful black walnut bureau, a large clothes closet, a table, chairs, a set of pots and skillets, knives, forks, spoons . . .

ABE, CAN YOU GRAB THE SPINNING WHEEL?

Intrigued, Abe ran his fingers over the wooden bureau, plunged his hands into the soft pillows. He had never felt such fine things. Was it possible—could it be—that life might get better for them?

As soon as she was settled, Sarah began putting her own stamp on the Lincoln cabin. She cast aside the rough old corn husks that Abe and his sister had been sleeping on. "These are fit for a pigpen," she declared, piling them in the yard. That night, Abe slept on a feathered mattress for the first time in his life.

"Bath time!" she proclaimed, and she proceeded to wash and rinse the grimy Lincoln children until they were as clean as her own.

There were changes in store for Thomas Lincoln as well. Sarah soon put him to work laying down a wood floor, patching the roof so the snow wouldn't pile up on the children's beds, and hanging a proper door to protect them from the elements. When Christmas came that year, the children feasted on wild turkey and venison, prepared in a well-stocked kitchen. They went to bed with warm blankets and full bellies.

Among all the kids in her blended family, Sarah took a special liking for Abe. She soon discovered that her new stepson was fond of reading. Although she was barely literate, she encouraged him to read and study as much as possible. To get him started, she gave him several books from her own collection, including *Aesop's Fables*, *Robinson Crusoe*, and *Sinbad the Sailor*.

Spurred on by his stepmother, Abe began to educate himself. He read in the fields. He read in the kitchen. He read in the woodpile while chopping wood. When he ran out of candles, he read by the light of a log fire.

He copied arithmetic problems onto the back of an old wooden shovel. When it was covered with figures, he scraped them off and started again.

In the back of one of his schoolbooks he penned the following rhyme:

Abraham Lincoln is my name
And with my pen I wrote the same
I wrote in both haste and speed
And left it here for fools to read

As a grown-up, Abraham Lincoln became well known for wise and witty sayings, like "A house divided against itself cannot stand," and for his moving speeches like "The Gettysburg Address." If not for the arrival of his not-so-wicked stepmother, he might never have nurtured his passion for language and learning.

Indeed, Sarah Johnston Lincoln enriched her son's life, making it possible for him to become first a state legislator, then a U.S. congressman, and finally the president of the United States. She cheered every great milestone of his political career and lived long enough to see him enter the White House. Although she was too old and frail to visit him, Abe remained close to her, always. He even kept a 40-acre plot of land for her to use at all times. As he once said, "All I am or ever hope to be, I owe to her".

DWIGHT
EISENHOWER

—— AND HIS ——

THREE
LESSONS OF
LEADERSHIP

=== BORN 1890 ===

In 1952, America said "I Like Ike" and elected this former army general as the nation's thirty-fourth president. Dwight Eisenhower may have seemed like a born commander, but his calm and confident manner came from years of hard work and careful study. Even as a kid, he was always learning new lessons in how to be a great leader.

Ike grew up in the town of Abilene, Kansas, and he learned his first leadership lesson on the first day of school. While exploring the playground for the first time, he drew the attention of a bigger boy who decided to test Ike's mettle. The boy began to chase Ike around the schoolyard, bellowing scary threats.

The bullying went on for a long time, until a third boy arrived on the scene. It was Ike's older brother, Arthur. Normally he was the quietest of the Eisenhower boys, but not that day. That day he was angry.

That day on the schoolyard, Ike learned an important lesson of leadership, one that he would apply many times as an adult.

Ike learned his second leadership lesson soon afterward, during a visit to his Uncle Luther's farm. He was heading outside to explore the barnyard when suddenly he heard a loud hissing noise. He looked up and saw a very large—and very angry—goose charging toward him!

Ike ran back to the safety of the house. Uncle Luther explained that the goose didn't like anyone "trespassing" on his territory.

"Thus the war began," Ike later remembered. For the rest of the day, every half hour or so, Ike would tiptoe out into the barnyard, hoping to get a good look at his adversary. Then, from out of nowhere, the goose would attack—*HISSSSS!*—and send him scurrying back to the kitchen door.

Ike was more determined than ever to cross the barnyard. But the goose refused to let him pass.

After Ike had beaten several hasty retreats, an un-expected ally came to his aid. Uncle Luther appeared, brandishing a worn-out broomstick with all the straw cut off. It was the perfect defense against a determined bird—enough to give him a good scare but not hurt him. The two of them headed out into the yard. After a few quick lessons, Ike learned to swing the broomstick for maximum effect. Then Uncle Luther patted him on his head and headed back inside. "You're on your own now, Ike," he said.

Ike was armed for battle, but how would the enemy react? He soon found out. The rampaging goose returned, even madder than before. It crept closer. Trembling, Ike stood his ground. Then, with a whooping war cry, he rushed at the goose, swinging the broom handle as hard as he could. The bird panicked, and when it turned tail to run away, Ike gave it a swift smack on the backside for good measure. "SQUAWWWK!" shrieked the goose as Ike chased it out of the barnyard.

After that, Ike never left his uncle's house without the broomstick. As for the goose, it kept its distance, hissing spitefully from the edge of the yard but never again daring to come any closer. Ike had shown the foul-tempered fowl who was boss, and in the process he learned another important lesson: "Never negotiate with an adversary except from a position of strength."

ALWAYS NEGOTIATE FROM A POSITION OF STRENGTH.

PUT DOWN THE STICK, WE'LL SEE HOW TOUGH YOU ARE.

Ike learned his third leadership lesson at age ten. After years of scrapping with bullies and ferocious farm animals, Ike had developed an explosive temper. He became used to getting what he wanted by fighting and often flew into a rage if he didn't get his way. One Halloween, his older brothers Arthur and Edgar went out trick-or-treating. Ike wanted to go with them, but his mother said he was too young.

SORRY, IKE, YOU HAVE TO STAY HOME TONIGHT.

SORRY, LITTLE BUCKAROO.

Ike threw the biggest tantrum of his life. Overtaken by resentment and anger toward his mother, he raced out into the yard and began to pound his fists against the bark of an old apple tree. He pummeled and thrashed until his knuckles were bloody; he was out of control. His father came out into the yard, grabbed his son by the shoulders, and sent him to his room.

About an hour later, Ike's mother came to visit. She found him crying into his pillow and sat beside him. She rubbed medicine onto his bruised knuckles and bandaged them up. Then she talked to him about anger and the importance of keeping it in check. She talked about hatred toward other people and how it can blind us to what's going on around us. She told Ike that he had the worst temper of all the Eisenhower brothers and would have to work the hardest to control it. Finally, she quoted from the Bible:

SNIFF

SNIFF

HE THAT CONQUERETH HIS OWN SOUL IS GREATER THAN HE WHO TAKETH A CITY.

KNUCKLE Salve

In other words, learn to control your emotions. Don't let your emotions take control of you.

Ike would later remember that conversation with his mother as one of the most important moments of his life. As a general, and then as president, he made it his policy never to get angry in public. He even came up with a novel way of "getting rid of" his negative emotions. Whenever somebody did something that displeased him, he would write the person's name on a piece of scrap paper and drop it into the lowest drawer of his desk. Then he would say to himself:

★ ★ ★

PRESIDENTIAL

REPORT

★ CARDS ★

THINK THERE'S NO SUCH THING AS A
"PERMANENT RECORD"?

THINK AGAIN.

Here are excerpts from report cards
and other teacher comments about
kids who grew up to be president.

"Quick in learning and still patient in study."

—Zachary Taylor's first teacher

"Terribly stubborn about many things. He would insist on having his way not only with me, but with his mother."

—Benjamin Harrison's childhood tutor

"Quiet demeanor, studious attention to his books, and remarkably good behavior."

—Ulysses S. Grant's teacher

"He will surely one day be a great professor, or, who knows, he may become even President of the United States."

—Theodore Roosevelt's foreign language instructor

"A fat little boy, always reading."

—Herbert Hoover's teacher

"He has been a thoroughly faithful scholar and a most satisfactory member of this school throughout his course."

—Franklin Delano Roosevelt's teacher

"He is casual and disorderly in almost all of his organization projects. Jack studies at the last minute, keeps appointments late, has little sense of material values, and can seldom locate his possessions."

—John F. Kennedy's teacher

"A very solemn child [who] rarely ever smiled or laughed."

—Richard Nixon's first-grade teacher

"A good student, cooperative. I can't say he was the smartest boy I've ever taught, but he was among the top ten."

—Jimmy Carter's first-grade teacher

―――――――――――――――――――――――――――――――

"When you grow up you're either going to be governor or get in a lot of trouble."

—Bill Clinton's sixth-grade teacher

―――――――――――――――――――――――――――――――

"An upstanding lad with great self-confidence. It appears, however, that he may be somewhat eccentric."

—George H. W. Bush's teacher

JOHN F. KENNEDY

AND THE

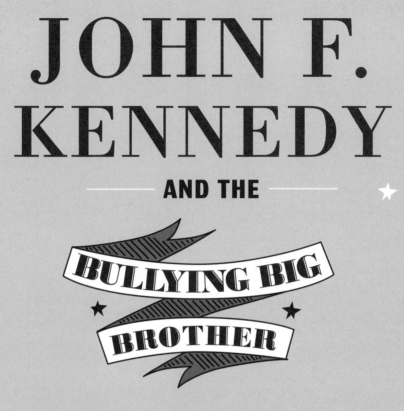

BULLYING BIG BROTHER

=== BORN 1917 ===

He was the youngest man ever elected U.S. president, but he was no kid. When he took office in 1961, John F. Kennedy had already survived a slew of childhood illnesses, fought in a war, and written a book about courageous American leaders. But the biggest challenge faced by "Jack" may have been escaping from the shadow of his older brother.

"If you bring up the eldest son right," Jack Kennedy's mother once explained, "that is very important because the younger ones watch him. If he works at his studies and his sports until he is praised, the others will follow his example."

That was certainly the rule in the Kennedy household. Oldest brother Joe got all the praise while the next-oldest, Jack, was treated like a pale copy of the original. From the time the boys were little, their father went around telling everybody that Joe would be president of the United States someday.

SOMEDAY JOE, YOU'LL BE PRESIDENT

HEY, WHAT ABOUT ME?

Eager to please his parents, Joe reveled in his role as "Golden Boy." But that didn't sit well with Jack. To him, Joe did not seem like a role model. He seemed like a bully.

When they played catch, Joe wouldn't throw the ball to Jack. He'd throw it *at* him.

When they played football, Joe liked to slam the ball hard into Jack's stomach, then laugh uproariously as his little brother doubled over in pain.

The brothers also staged epic wrestling matches. Joe used his superior size and strength to easily pin Jack to the canvas.

One time, when the boys were playing on the beach, Jack put on Joe's bathing suit by mistake. Joe grew enraged and chased Jack into the ocean, where he tackled him and began fighting him as the waves crashed around them. A family friend had to break them up before either was seriously hurt.

And then there was the disastrous bike race. One day, Joe challenged his brother to cycle around the neighborhood. Each took off from the same spot headed in opposite directions. They pedaled furiously around the block to see who could return to the starting line first.

As the competitors sped toward the finish, it looked like anybody's race. But neither brother was willing to concede defeat. Instead of stopping, they collided head-on.

Joe walked away without a scratch. Jack was not so lucky. His injuries resulted in twenty-eight stitches. "At least I showed him I won't back down," Jack told himself.

Jack took every opportunity to exact even a small measure of revenge on his rival. At dinner one night, Joe was served his favorite meal of roast beef with orange meringue. As usual, the other Kennedy kids had to wait until Joe's plate was filled before digging into their own. Seeing his chance, Jack dove across the table, snatched the beef from Joe's plate, and stuffed into his own mouth. A full-on, two-fisted brawl broke out.

But Jack's moments of triumph were few and far between. Indeed, Joe's status within the family only grew.
When their father was often away on business, young
Joe stood in for him as head of the household. At dinner, he sat at the head of the table, carving knife in hand,
and meted out punishments to the other children. "I'm in
charge!" he'd gleefully declare whenever Joe Sr. left town.

SORRY JACK,
NO TURKEY —
FOR YOU!

And the crazy thing was, Jack's younger siblings seemed to love their brother Joe! They didn't consider him a bully; because their real father was often out of town, Joe was the next best thing. He spent many hours playing catch with his younger brother Bobby or swimming with their youngest brother, Teddy. He cheered on his sisters at their sporting events and taught them all how to sail. Whenever Joe returned home from school, the younger siblings would run over and jump in his arms, just as they did when their father came home.

It took a long time, but eventually Jack came to see Joe in a new light, although they never became close. One year, when Joe went away to camp, Jack briefly assumed the duties as head of the household in their father's absence. By summer's end, Jack was begging Joe Sr. to let him go to camp with Joe the next year. The responsibility of being a role model was too tough to bear.

By the time he was a young adult, Jack understood that the pressure of living up to Joe's example had taught him important lessons: how to be tough, how to compete, and how to win. He followed Joe to college, then on to law school, and then into military service. At each step, Jack's achievements exceeded those of his older brother, something even his demanding parents could not fail to notice.

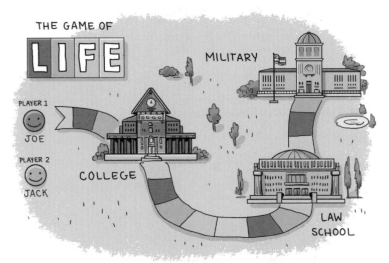

In 1944, Joe was killed in action while on a dangerous bombing mission during World War II. He was only twenty-nine years old. It then fell to Jack, the next oldest of the nine Kennedy children, to fulfill their father's dream and become president of the United States.

Which is exactly what happened. John F. Kennedy entered the White House on January 20, 1961, when he was just forty-three years old (making him the youngest president ever elected to office). He helped advance the U.S. space program and inspired Americans to work together to send the first man to the moon. Today, many polls still rank him as one of America's most popular presidents.

As an adult, John F. Kennedy admitted that he owed a lot of his success to his big brother Joe. Yes, they fought like crazy, and at times they seemed to hate each other. But the constant competition inspired the younger Kennedy to work harder, play faster, and study longer.

In a book of reminiscences about his older brother, he wrote the following:

Joe did many things well...but I have always felt that Joe achieved his greatest success as the oldest brother. Very early in life he acquired a sense of responsibility towards his brothers and sisters, and I do not think that he ever forgot it.

I think that if the Kennedy children...ever amount to anything, it will be due more to Joe's behavior and his constant example than to any other factor.

LYNDON JOHNSON

CLASS CLOWN

BORN 1908

Even a class clown can grow up to do great things. Lyndon B. Johnson accomplished a lot during his five years as America's president. Nothing pleased him more than signing laws designed to help students and teachers. But few who knew this classroom cut-up as a kid could have predicted he would one day become America's first "education president."

The first time Lyndon saw his schoolteacher, Miss Kate Deadrich, he fell head over heels in love. He followed her around the school, clinging to her skirts. "Miss Kate, I don't like you one bit," he announced one day. "I just love you!"

HOW I LONG TO SCALE THE DIZZYING HEIGHTS OF YOUR MAJESTIC CLIFFS, MY TOWERING PARAMOUR!

Miss Kate was the only teacher at the Junction School, a one-room schoolhouse in rural Texas. Thirty students sat in two rows of double desks—boys in one row, girls in another. Most were German immigrants who didn't speak English. They had certainly never seen anyone quite like Lyndon Johnson.

Lyndon tried everything to get attention from his classmates—and from Miss Kate. He was full of surprises. Even though the school was an easy walk from his family's farm, Lyndon often traveled there via donkey. Sometimes he dressed in outrageous costumes, including one time in a white sailor suit and another in a cowboy outfit with a ten-gallon hat.

THIS IS WAY BETTER THAN TAKING THE SCHOOL BUS!

SCHOOL

Lyndon was always coming up with new ways to act out and misbehave. One day, Miss Kate asked him to read from a book to his classmates. To her astonishment, he refused. He just stood in front of the class, silent, even though his teacher knew he read better than most of the other children. This happened again and again until finally Miss Kate turned to Lyndon's mother for advice. Mrs. Johnson explained that her son just wanted more attention, and she suggested that Miss Kate try letting Lyndon sit on her lap. The strategy worked—and from that day forward, whenever Miss Kate wanted Lyndon to read, she had to lift the boy onto her lap.

But when Lyndon realized his bad behavior was being rewarded, his pranks worsened.

One day a boy named Hugo Klein brought a slice of lemon meringue pie to school for lunch. While Hugo was playing outside during recess, Lyndon opened Hugo's lunchbox and devoured the dessert. Then he sauntered onto the playground with lemon meringue dripping off his face. "I got me some pie!" he crowed, even as Hugo started to cry.

On another occasion, Lyndon was asked to write his name on the blackboard. He obeyed but he wrote in huge capital letters across two blackboards: LYN-DON B. on one and JOHNSON on the other.

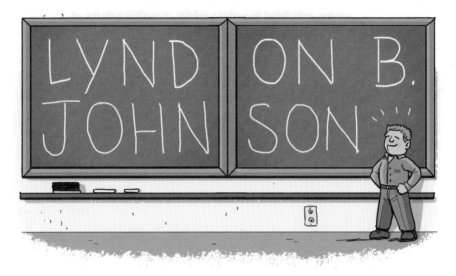

His parents were at their wit's end. Every night, his father would come home from work and ask the same question: "Well, what has Lyndon done today?" While Mrs. Johnson listed his many acts of mischief, Lyndon would hide by the kitchen stove, hoping to avoid punishment.

... AND THEN HE DIPPED THE CAT IN PEANUT BUTTER, AND THEN HE SET THE COUCH ON FIRE, AND THEN...

The most remarkable thing about this story isn't that this prankster grew up to be president of the United States. There are plenty of presidents who misbehaved in elementary school (see the story about Bill Clinton on page 58, for instance).

No, the remarkable thing is that Lyndon Johnson grew up to be a teacher! Soon after he finished college, he was hired to teach at the Welhausen Elementary School in Cotulla, Texas. It was a small red-brick schoolhouse similar to the one he had attended as a child. And many of his students were like little Lyndons—they were constantly using recess time to fight, pull pranks, and misbehave.

The new teacher laid down strict rules for his class: no laughing and no joking. Any student who didn't complete the assigned homework had to stay after school.

In the mornings, Lyndon would walk up and down the rows of his classroom, asking if students had done their lessons. If any answered "No," he would pinch their ears until they squealed. He seemed to understand the discipline kids needed to stay out of trouble. He improved the sports program and helped organize many after-school activities: band, track, a debating society, a spelling bee, and a talent show. As a result, he quickly became the most popular teacher in school. Sometimes his students would greet him with a special song.

The lyrics went something like this:

How do you do, Mr. Johnson,
How do you do?
How do you do, Mr. Johnson,
How are you?
We'll do it if we can,
We'll stand by you to a man,
How do you do, Mr. Johnson?

Lyndon Johnson was soon made principal of the entire school. And he never forgot the lessons he learned there—or the value of a good education.

When he became president some thirty years later, Lyndon Johnson signed more than sixty education bills into law. One of the most important was the Elementary and Secondary Education Act, which provided funds for libraries, textbooks, and school breakfasts. When it came time to sign the document, Johnson returned to the Junction School, where he had once been the infamous "class troublemaker."

By his side was Miss Kate. The president joked about how he had learned to read while sitting on her lap before putting his pen to paper. "As president of the United States, I believe deeply no law that I have signed, or will ever sign, means more to the future of America," he said. Then he handed the pen to his former teacher.

YOU WERE A BAD BOY, LYNDON, BUT YOU'RE A GOOD PRESIDENT.

GERALD FORD

THE ANGRIEST BOY IN THE WORLD

BORN 1913

He never expected to be president. But when Richard Nixon resigned from office, Gerald Ford took over, and America held its breath waiting to see if the new leader was up to the job. Though others may have doubted him, Ford always had faith in himself. He'd overcome many obstacles in his life. Being the most powerful man in the world turned out to be one of the easy ones.

Gerald "Junie" Ford was boiling mad. Those meddling twins were at it again. The two girls, Marian and Alice Steketee, had rounded up the neighborhood kids and brought them to play in his backyard. In *his* yard, with *his* cherry tree! He was outnumbered. The twins were twice his age. But he stormed up and yelled at them anyway.

This wasn't Junie's first argument with other children, and it wouldn't be his last. In fact, he had the worst temper of any kid in his neighborhood.

And anger wasn't his only problem. Around the time he turned seven, Junie developed a terrible stutter. He could form the beginnings of words, but he couldn't say the endings. He began to lose confidence, and that made him even angrier.

Junie's mother tried everything to keep her son from throwing temper tantrums. She would punish him by twisting his ear or sending him to his room. But nothing seemed to work.

One day, after an especially bad fit, Junie's mom took him aside and gave him a poem by an English writer named Rudyard Kipling. "Read this," she said. "It will help you control that temper of yours." Junie eyed the paper suspiciously. The poem was called "If," and it began with these words:

If you can keep your head when all about you
Are losing theirs and blaming it on you...

Hmmm, it sounded like a personal message to Junie. He kept reading:

If you can trust yourself when all men doubt you
But make allowance for their doubting too...

Junie realized that his mother was trying to tell him something. The best people keep calm when bad things happened. They didn't lose their cool. It made sense.

IF YOU CAN KEEP YOUR HEAD WHEN ALL ABOUT YOU ARE LOSING THEIRS...

From that day forward, whenever Junie got up-set, his mother would have him repeat the poem—the whole text, from beginning to end—until he calmed down. After repeating it many, many times, he eventually took the poem's message to heart. Soon, his fits of fury ended.

As for his stuttering, that seemed to disappear on its own—and Junie was much older before he understood why. The reason had to do with penmanship. See, Junie Ford was left-handed, a quality that today we don't find unusual. (About one in ten people are natuarally left-handed.)

But back in the 1920s, teachers would try to turn "left-ies" into "righties" by forbidding left-handed kids from writing with their dominant (left) hand. Junie's teachers forced him to copy long passages of text with his right hand. The work was frustrating and may have fueled a lot of his outbursts. Coincidentally, he started stuttering around the same time as he was learning to write.

I will not write with my left hand.   I will not write with my left hand.
I will not write with my left hand.   I will not write with my left hand.
I will not write with my left hand.   I will not write with my left hand.
I will not write with my left hand.   I will not write with my left hand.
I will not write with my left hand.   I will not write with my left hand.
I will not write with my left hand.   I will not write with my left hand.
I will not write with my left hand.   I will not write with my left hand.

Today, many scientists believe that writing with the "wrong" hand flips a switch in the brain that triggers a speech impediment. Once you flip the switch back, over time the problem corrects itself. As soon as Junie's teachers allowed him to write with his left hand, his speech improved. The stutter vanished and his confidence returned.

The angriest boy in the world went on to become one of the best-liked kids in his high school. He was a straight-A student, an eagle scout, and a star football player. In college, he graduated near the top of his class.

According to those who knew him best, there's one thing Gerald Ford never did as president: he never lost his cool. He'd stopped getting angry a long time ago.

RELAX! I'M SURE IF WE KEEP OUR HEADS WE CAN SOLVE THIS PROBLEM.

RONALD REAGAN

NEAR-SIGHTED SUPERHERO

BORN 1911

Whether uniting America's allies or negotiating with its enemies, the president they called "the Great Communicator" never met a person he couldn't persuade. But Ronald Reagan wasn't always so confident. In fact, if he hadn't learned to set aside his pride and pick up a pair of eyeglasses, he might never have made it to the White House.

As a kid, **Ronald Reagan** couldn't see straight. When he was little, his parents made him get his hair cut so that his bangs grew down over his eyes. The style was called a "Dutch boy." Whenever his bangs grew too long, the barber chopped a tiny hole in the hair helmet so that he could peep out.

To make matters worse, now everyone called him "the little Dutchman," or "Dutch" for short.

Like most kids, Dutch got into his share of misadventures. Once, when fooling around with some fireworks, he launched a rocket into the side of a bridge. He was hauled down to the local police station and forced to pay a fine. Another time, he was goofing off by railroad tracks when a steam train started to roll out of the station and nearly ran right over him.

But mostly he kept to himself, playing quietly in his room with his army of tin soldiers or reading books about natural history. His favorite one was about wolves, which he read so many times that, years later, he could still recite it word for word from memory. And then there was his prized butterfly and birds' egg collection.

Dutch had stumbled upon the collection by accident. When he was about six years old, his family moved to a new house in Galesburg, Illinois. One day he crept up into the dusty attic. There, enclosed in a glass case, was a magnificent array of birds' eggs and preserved butterflies. It had been left behind by the home's previous owner—and now it was all his. Dutch spent hours alone in the attic, marveling at the spectacular colors of the eggs and the intricate patterns on the butterfly wings. Many years later, when he was governor of California, he signed a bill making the dog-face butterfly the state's official state insect. He never lost his sense of wonder about the natural world.

But there was another reason Dutch liked hobbies involving the close-up study of small things: he was severely near-sighted.

When it came to seeing anything more than a few feet away, Dutch's eyesight was horrible. To him, a tree on the side of the road looked like a green blob. A billboard was nothing but a gigantic fuzzy rectangle. In school, Dutch would have to take a seat in the front of the class to see the blackboard. Most of the time, he had no idea what was written on it. When his schoolmates chose sides for baseball, he was always the last one picked.

He couldn't see a pitch until it was almost on him. He was conked on the head more times than he could count. It was maddening, frightening, and embarrassing.

That all ended one Sunday afternoon when Dutch was about thirteen years old. That day, he went for a drive in the country with his parents. His mother accidentally left her eyeglasses on the backseat. On a lark,

Dutch picked them up and put them on. In that instant, everything changed. He let out a yell so loud that his father nearly drove off the road.

The trees! They suddenly had branches—and leaves! The billboards had words on them! The world had a beautiful and astonishing clarity he'd never seen before.

The fields beyond the roadside were filled with heavy, brown, lazily chewing creatures that had to be dairy cows. "Look!" Dutch exclaimed, pointing out the window to a spot where a herd was grazing. It was as if a whole new world had magically opened before his blinking eyes.

The next day, Dutch went to an eye doctor. He was told he had 20/200 vision, meaning that he was legally blind.

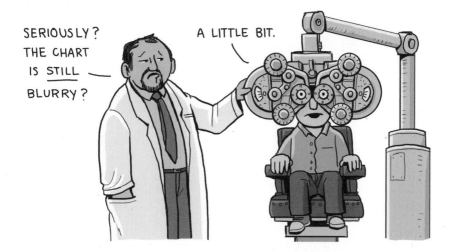

He was immediately fitted for a pair of huge, thick, black horn-rimmed eyeglasses. They were ugly and he hated wearing them. But they gave him something he never had before: confidence.

Now that he could see clearly, Dutch threw himself into sports and physical fitness. He had always been a good swimmer, but now he felt comfortable enough to try out for a job as a lifeguard. He took a lifesaving course at the YMCA and was hired as a volunteer lifeguard on an especially treacherous section of the Rock River, which ran through his hometown.

For the next seven summers, Dutch worked twelve hours a day, seven days a week, from Memorial Day to Labor Day. He kept his glasses in his lifeguard chair at all times. When swimmers strayed out too far, or stayed too long in the water, he would throw pebbles at them and shout out, "River rat!"

That usually got their attention. Sometimes it didn't, however, and Dutch would have to dive in and pull them to safety.

Every time Dutch rescued someone, he carved a notch in a wooden log on the river's edge. After seven summers, there were seventy-seven notches on the log—one for each of the lives he had saved.

And it wasn't just people he rescued. One time, an old man offered Dutch ten dollars to dive into the river and retrieve his false teeth, which had fallen out while he was swimming. It took Dutch several tries, but he finally found them. That was his first paying job.

Years later, one of Ronald Reagan's biographers wrote that working as a lifeguard left him with a lifelong desire to save people. That idea was proven true on an especially memorable occasion. On July 4, 1967, Reagan was in his first term as governor of California. During a Fourth of July pool party at his home, the young daughter of one of his guests was having trouble swimming. Noticing her distress, Reagan excused himself from the party and leapt into the pool—clothes and all—to rescue her from drowning.

So the final tally of lives saved by the man who would one day become America's fortieth president is seventy-eight. Not bad for a near-sighted butterfly collector from Dixon, Illinois.

45 FACTS
ABOUT
45
PRESIDENTS

★ ★ ★

WE COULDN'T FIT A CHAPTER ON EVERY
PRESIDENT IN THIS BOOK, BUT WE HATE TO
LEAVE ANY OUT. HERE'S A BONUS FACT ABOUT
EACH OF AMERICA'S KID PRESIDENTS.

AND YES,
WE COUNTED GROVER CLEVELAND TWICE,
BECAUSE HE SERVED TWO SEPARATE
TERMS IN THE WHITE HOUSE!

GEORGE WASHINGTON was really bad at spelling.

JOHN ADAMS brought his musket to school every morning so that he could go hunting in the woods immediately after class.

THOMAS JEFFERSON's best friend was an enslaved man named Jupiter.

By the age of eleven, **JAMES MADISON** had read all eighty-five books in his father's library. By age sixteen, he could read the works of philosophers like Plato and Aristotle in the original Greek.

One of **JAMES MONROE**'s best friends was the future Supreme Court chief justice John Marshall.

When he was nine years old, JOHN QUINCY ADAMS watched the Battle of Bunker Hill from his backyard.

ANDREW JACKSON was the first president to be born in a log cabin.

MARTIN VAN BUREN helped popularize the expression "OK." The initials stand for "Old Kinderhook," the name of his hometown.

WILLIAM HENRY HARRISON's father signed the Declaration of Independence.

JOHN TYLER's father was close friends with Thomas Jefferson.

JAMES K. POLK learned to ride a horse before he learned to walk.

ZACHARY TAYLOR once swam across the Ohio River and back again.

MILLARD FILLMORE taught himself to read by studying the dictionary.

When he was eleven years old, FRANKLIN PIERCE was sent away to boarding school. He grew so homesick that he decided to return home—fourteen miles, on foot—to have Sunday dinner with his family.

JAMES BUCHANAN was born with an eye defect that made one of his eyelids twitch and forced him to cock his head to the left when talking to someone. A historian once referred to him as a "winking, fidgeting little busybody."

At age ten, ABRAHAM LINCOLN was kicked in the head by a horse and almost died.

ANDREW JOHNSON worked twelve hours a day as an apprentice in a tailor shop. He learned to read by listening to customers read aloud to him while he sewed their clothes.

When he was seven, ULYSSES S. GRANT fell into a creek while fishing and nearly drowned. A friend pulled him out of the water just in time.

RUTHERFORD B. HAYES's mother wouldn't let him go outside until he was five years old.

JAMES GARFIELD was the last president to be born in a log cabin.

CHESTER ALAN ARTHUR's middle name is pronounced *a-LAN*.

GROVER CLEVELAND worked as a clerk in a general store. His salary was fifty dollars a year.

BENJAMIN HARRISON's mother once wrote him a letter advising him never to eat cucumbers.

GROVER CLEVELAND used to sneak out at night and pull the gates off people's fences.

WILLIAM MCKINLEY liked to walk around barefoot, even in cold weather. He used to warm his feet by pressing them into the dirt where cows had slept.

THEODORE ROOSEVELT's asthma was so bad, he had to sleep sitting up in a chair in order to breathe.

When his brothers fought, WILLIAM HOWARD TAFT served as the referee.

WOODROW WILSON's backyard was used as a Confederate prison camp during the Civil War. Woodrow and his cousin Jessie liked to sneak in and talk with the Union Army soldiers imprisoned there.

WARREN G. HARDING was a member of a gang called the Stunners.

CALVIN COOLIDGE was painfully shy. When he heard the sound of a stranger's voice in the house, he ran away and hid.

HERBERT HOOVER's favorite book was *David Copperfield* by Charles Dickens.

While on a bicycling tour of Germany, fourteen-year-old FRANKLIN D. ROOSEVELT got arrested four times in one day.

He ran over a goose, picked cherries from a tree without permission, parked his bike at a train station, and was cited for cycling after sunset.

||||||||||||||||||||||||||||||||||||||||||||||||||||||||||||||||||||||||||||||||||||||||||||||||||||

HARRY S TRUMAN is one of seventeen presidents who don't have a middle name. The "S" doesn't stand for anything and so doesn't have a period after it.

||||||||||||||||||||||||||||||||||||||||||||||||||||||||||||||||||||||||||||||||||||||||||||||||||||

DWIGHT D. EISENHOWER had five brothers, all of whom were known by the nickname "Ike."

||||||||||||||||||||||||||||||||||||||||||||||||||||||||||||||||||||||||||||||||||||||||||||||||||||

JOHN F. KENNEDY was so skinny, the kids at school called him "Rat Face."

||||||||||||||||||||||||||||||||||||||||||||||||||||||||||||||||||||||||||||||||||||||||||||||||||||

LYNDON JOHNSON had such big floppy earlobes that kids would pay him a nickel to yank on them until he started crying.

When he was fourteen years old, RICHARD NIXON worked as a carnival barker at the Slippery Gulch Rodeo.

GERALD FORD found out that he was adopted when he was twelve years old.

JIMMY CARTER developed a strong distaste for sauerkraut after one of his teachers served it to him for lunch.

RONALD REAGAN and a friend once ate four pounds of spare ribs in one sitting.

GEORGE H. W. BUSH and his brother Prescott fought so much that their mother offered each boy his own bedroom. After a "trial separation," the feuding boys decided they preferred rooming together.

BILL CLINTON once found a snake living in the family outhouse.

GEORGE W. BUSH was the head cheer-leader in his high school.

||||||||||||||||||||||||||||||||||||||||||||||||||||||||||||||||||||||||||||||||||||||||||||

BARACK OBAMA's third-grade teacher asked him to write an essay entitled "What I Want to Be in the Future." He wrote:

My name is Barry Soetoro. I am a third-grade student at SD Asisi.
    My mom is my idol.
    My teacher is Ibu Fer. I have a lot of friends.
    I live near the school. I usually walk to the school with my mom, then go home by myself.
    Someday I want to be president. I love to visit all the places in Indonesia.
    Done.
    The eeeeeeeend.

||||||||||||||||||||||||||||||||||||||||||||||||||||||||||||||||||||||||||||||||||||||||||||

As a boy, **DONALD TRUMP** took secret excursions into Manhattan to explore the big city. When his father learned of the trips, he sent Donald to a military boarding school.

AND THAT'S

THE

EEEEEEEEEEND

OF

★ ★ ★ **KID** ★ ★ ★
PRESIDENTS

THANKS
FOR READING!

★

PART I

AFTER-SCHOOL ACTIVITIES

You can read more about Ulysses Grant and his love of horses in *Ulysses S. Grant* by Jean Kinney Williams (Compass Point Books, 2003).

Theodore Roosevelt's many adventures are chronicled in *Teddy Roosevelt: American Rough Rider* by John Garraty (Sterling, 2007).

Relive Richard Nixon's hardscrabble boyhood in the pages of *Richard M. Nixon* by Herón Márquez (Lerner Publications, 2003), part of the Presidential Leaders series.

Learn all about Jimmy Carter's path to the White House—and read excerpts from his speeches—in *Jimmy Carter: On the Road to Peace* by Caroline Lazo (Silver Burdett Press, 1996).

The life of Bill Clinton is memorably told in *Bill Clinton: America's 42nd President* by Sean McCollum (Children's Press, 2005).

★

★

PART II

FANTASTIC JOURNEYS

George Washington may not have chopped down a cherry tree, but he did a lot of other interesting things. Read all about his exploits in *Who Was George Washington?* by Roberta Edwards (Grosset & Dunlap, 2009).

For more about the Revolutionary War experiences of Andrew Jackson, check out *Andrew Jackson: Young Patriot* by George E. Stanley (Aladdin, 2003).

The difficult childhood of America's thirty-first president is recounted in *Herbert Hoover* by Amy Ruth (Lerner Publishing Group, 2003).

Colorful illustrations help tell the story of Franklin D. Roosevelt's early life in *A Boy Named FDR* by Kathleen Krull (Alfred A. Knopf, 2010).

If you want to know more about Barack Obama's upbringing in Indonesia and Hawaii, you should read *Barack Obama: Son of Promise, Child of Hope* by Nikki Grimes (Simon & Schuster Books for Young Readers, 2008).

★

★

PART III

IT'S NOT EASY GROWING UP

There are a lot of good biographies about Abraham Lincoln. One of the best ones for kids is *Abraham Lincoln: A Photographic Story of a Life* by Tanya Lee Stone (DK Publishing, 2005).

If you like Ike, then you should definitely read the illustrated biography *Dwight D. Eisenhower* by Elaine Marie Alphin and Arthur B. Alphin (Lerner Publishing Group; 2004).

One of the best books about President Kennedy is *Jack: The Early Years of John F. Kennedy* by Ilene Cooper (Puffin, 2003).

You can learn all about Lyndon Johnson's accomplishments—and his misbehavior in school—in *Great Society: The Story of Lyndon Baines Johnson* by Nancy A. Colbert (Morgan Reynolds Publishing, 2002).

All the best stories from Gerald Ford's early life are collected in *Young Jerry Ford: Athlete and Citizen* by Hendrik Booraem V (Wm. B. Eerdmans, 2013).

★

Ronald Reagan is another president who's been the subject of many good biographies. One that focuses specifically on his childhood in Illinois is *Ronald Reagan: Young Leader* by Montrew Dunham (Aladdin, 1999). It's part of the Childhood of Famous Americans series.

INDEX

Ford, Gerald R., 7, 179–186, 205, 210

ACKNOWLEDGMENTS

★ **DAVID STABLER** would like to thank Rick Chillot, Blair Thornburgh, and Hanna Fogel for their able assistance with research; Doogie Horner and Mario Zucca for their beautiful illustrations; David Smith; Gary Teubner; Jaleel White; the staff of the Brooklyn Public Library; and Jason Rekulak, whose creative vision and editorial acumen inspired and improved this book at every turn.

★ **DOOGIE HORNER** would like to thank Jason Rekulak, David Stabler, and all the good people at Quirk Books. Special thanks to Mario Zucca for elevating my scribbles with his beautiful coloring, and to my dad for making me watch so many Civil War documentaries. And also, of course, Jennie.